LET'S READ MAPS!

PHYSICAL MAPS

by Adrianne Velasco

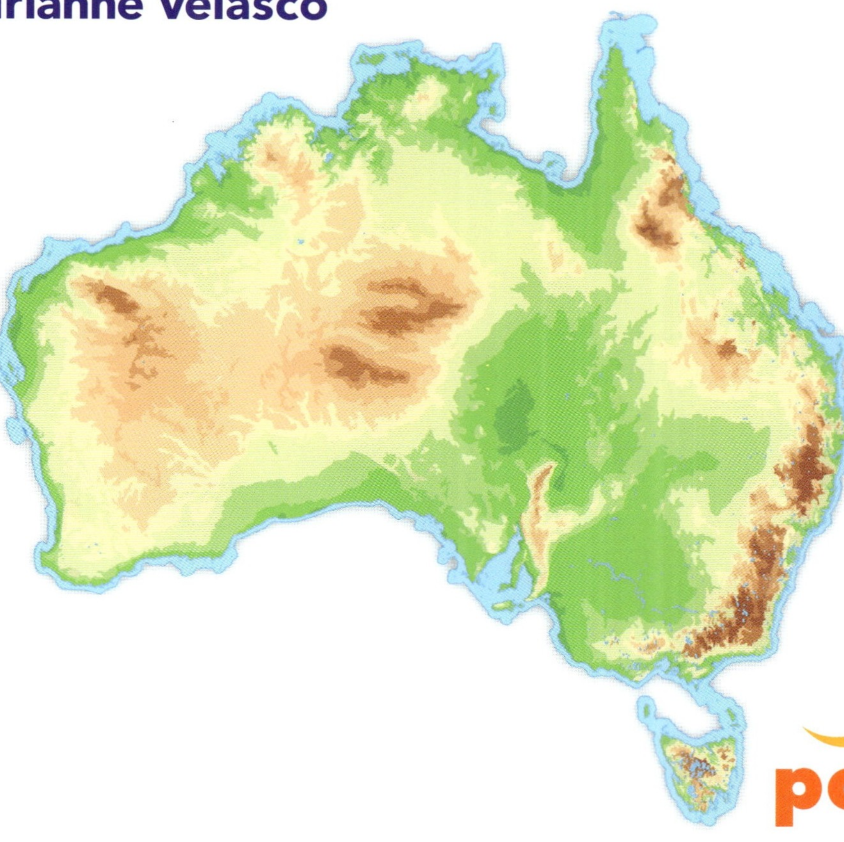

pogo

Ideas for Parents and Teachers

Pogo Books let children practice reading informational text while introducing them to nonfiction features such as headings, labels, sidebars, maps, and diagrams, as well as a table of contents, glossary, and index.

Carefully leveled text with a strong photo match offers early fluent readers the support they need to succeed.

Before Reading

- "Walk" through the book and point out the various nonfiction features. Ask the student what purpose each feature serves.
- Look at the glossary together. Read and discuss the words.

During Reading

- Have the child read the book independently.
- Invite them to list questions that arise from reading.

After Reading

- Discuss the child's questions. Talk about how they might find answers to those questions.
- Prompt the child to think more. Ask: Have you seen a physical map? What did it show you?

Pogo Books are published by Jump!
3500 American Blvd W, Suite 150
Bloomington, MN 55431
www.jumplibrary.com

Jump! is a division of FlutterBee Education Group.

Library of Congress Cataloging-in-Publication Data

Names: Velasco, Adrianne, author.
Title: Physical maps / by Adrianne Velasco.
Description: Minneapolis, MN: Jump!, Inc., [2026]
Series: Let's read maps! | Includes index.
Audience: Ages 7-10
Identifiers: LCCN 2024054510 (print)
LCCN 2024054511 (ebook)
ISBN 9798892139243 (hardcover)
ISBN 9798892139250 (paperback)
ISBN 9798892139267 (ebook)
Subjects: LCSH: Map reading–Juvenile literature.
Topographic maps–Juvenile literature.
Classification: LCC GA130 .V45 2026 (print
LCC GA130 (ebook)
DDC 912.01/4–dc23/eng/20250131
LC record available at https://lccn.loc.gov/2024054510
LC ebook record available at https://lccn.loc.gov/2024054511

Editor: Jenna Gleisner
Designer: Emma Almgren-Bersie

Photo Credits: bogdanserban/iStock, cover, 12-13; Adobe Stock, 1; Mlyons/iStock, 3; Wand_Prapan/iStock, 4; Roman Kybus/iStock, 5 (compass rose); Valentin Agapov/Shutterstock, 5 (paper); Venture Stone Creator/Shutterstock, 5 (background); Shutterstock, 6-7; dikobraziy/iStock, 8-9, 14-15; Oldesign/Shutterstock, 10-11; Hammad Khan/iStock, 16; Stramyk Igor/Adobe Stock, 17; DINphotogallery/iStock, 18-19; AnnaStills/iStock, 20-21; a7880ss/Adobe Stock, 23.

Printed in the United States of America at Corporate Graphics in North Mankato, Minnesota.

TABLE OF CONTENTS

CHAPTER 1

WHAT IS A MAP?

A map is a drawing of an area and its **features**. We can read a map to find out where we are. It can show us where to go.

Maps have tools to help us read them. A compass rose shows directions. It tells us which way is north (N), east (E), south (S), and west (W).

Maps are small drawings of large areas. A scale shows how big or far apart things are in real life. One inch (2.5 centimeters) on a map could be 150 miles (240 kilometers) in real life.

Latitude lines and **longitude lines** make a **grid**. They help us find exact places.

WHAT DO YOU THINK?

A map can be of your yard, city, or state. It can be of the entire world. A map could also show where to find treasure! If you could draw a map, what would it show? Why?

SCALE
1 inch (2.5 cm) = 150 miles (240 km)
longitude line
latitude line
N
W
E
S

CHAPTER 2

PHYSICAL MAP FEATURES

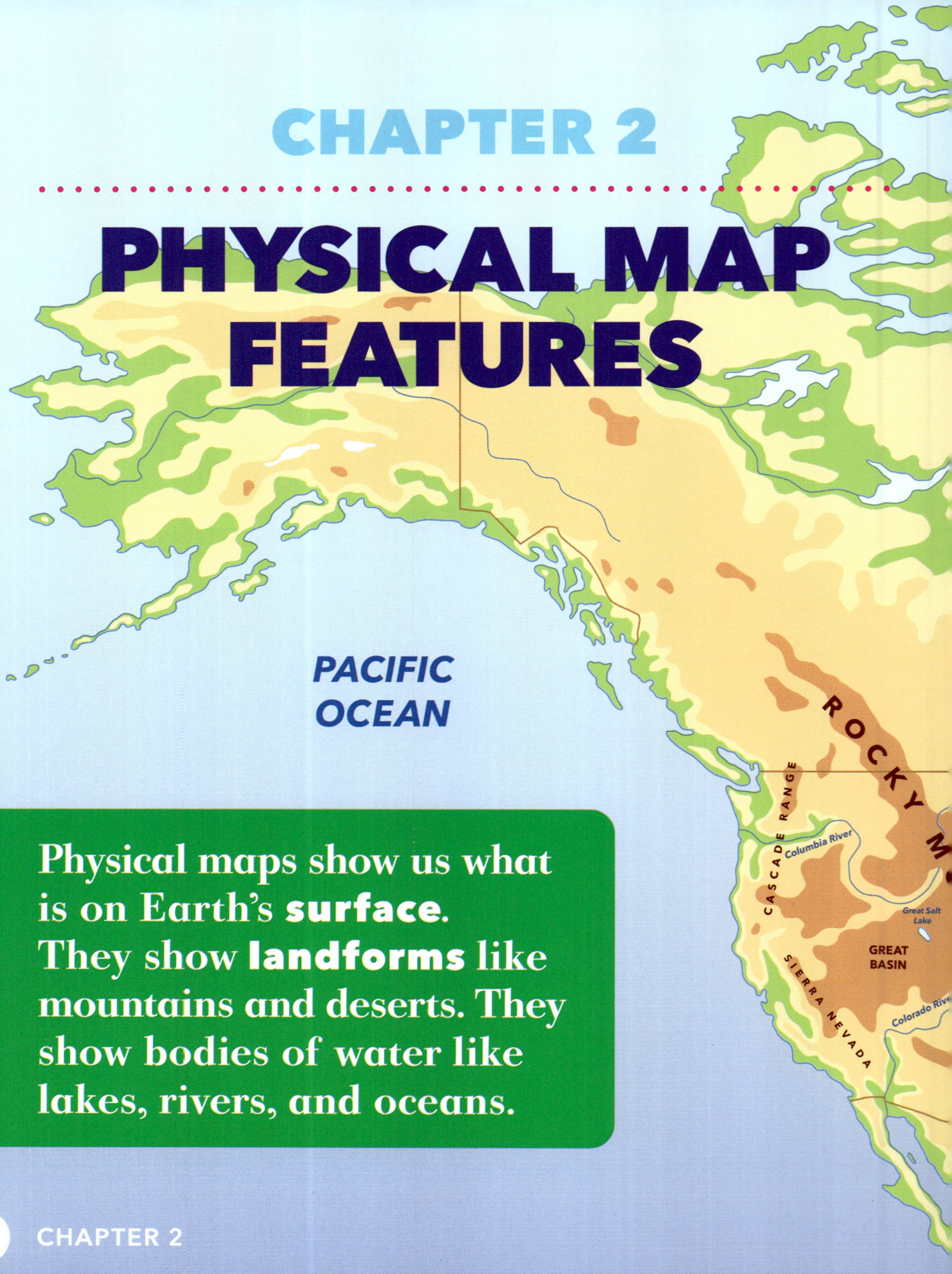

Physical maps show us what is on Earth's **surface**. They show **landforms** like mountains and deserts. They show bodies of water like lakes, rivers, and oceans.

MAP KEY
river
lake
Lake Superior
Missouri River
GREAT PLAINS
Mississippi River
Lake Huron
Lake Michigan
Lake Ontario
Lake Erie
Platte River
Ohio River
APPALACHIAN MOUNTAINS
Mississippi River
Rio Grande
ATLANTIC OCEAN
N
W
E
S

Physical maps use **symbols**. A map key tells us what the symbols mean. A triangle is used for mountains. A blue line is used for a river.

TAKE A LOOK!

What are common symbols on a physical map? What do they stand for? Take a look!

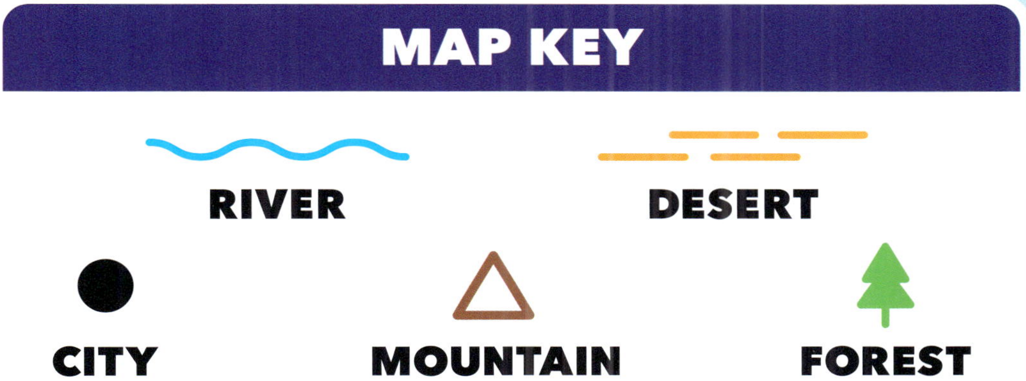

Physical maps show elevation. Elevation is how high something is above **sea level**. It is shown on maps with color shades. The lowest points on land are dark green. As land rises, the color changes. Dark green changes to light green, then yellow, brown, and dark brown.

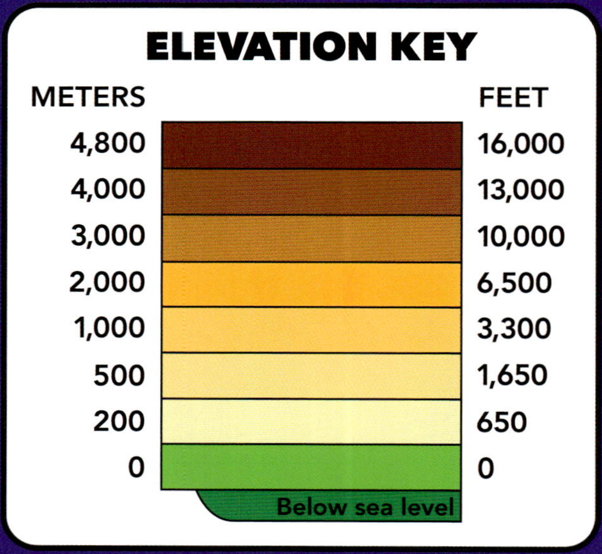

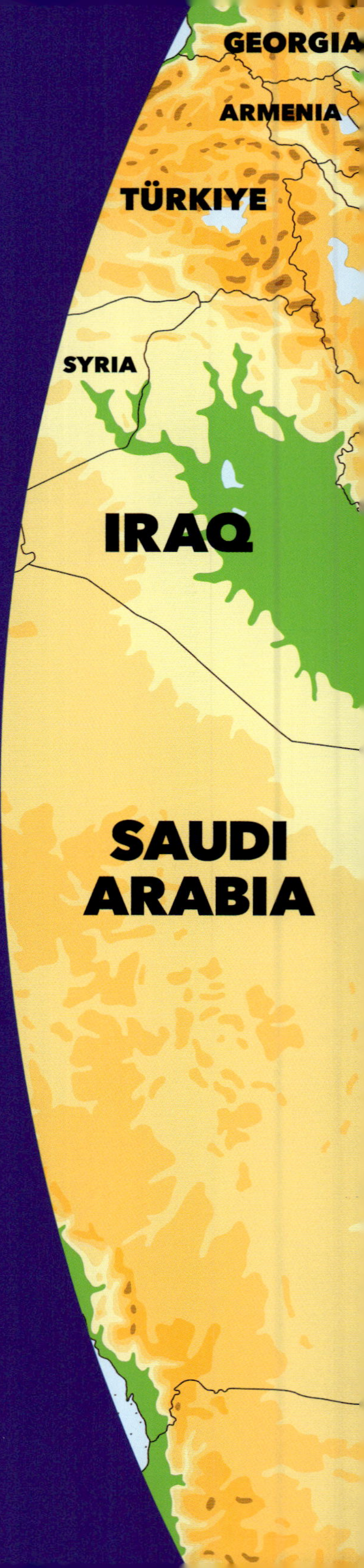

UZBEKISTAN
KYRGYZSTAN
CHINA
TAJIKISTAN
TURKMENISTAN
CASPIAN SEA
AFGHANISTAN
IRAN
PAKISTAN
PERSIAN GULF
OMAN
QATAR
INDIA
UNITED ARAB EMIRATES
ARABIAN SEA
OMAN
N
W
E
S
YEMEN

PACIFIC
OCEAN
INDIAN
OCEAN
SOUTHERN
OCEAN

Shades of blue show how deep water is. The deepest parts of the ocean are dark blue. Shallow parts are light blue.

WHAT DO YOU THINK?

Look at the colors of a physical map. Why do you think land colors are green, yellow, and brown? Why do you think water is shown in shades of blue?

ELEVATION KEY

METERS	FEET
4,800	16,000
3,600	12,000
2,000	6,500
200	650
0	0
-200	-650
-1,000	-3,300
-2,000	-6,500
-4,000	-13,000

CHAPTER 3

TYPES OF PHYSICAL MAPS

There are different kinds of physical maps. A relief map shows hills and valleys. It uses light and shadows. This creates a 3D effect. The higher the elevation, the darker the shading.

Topographic maps show the shape of Earth's features. How? They use contour lines. These show how high or low the elevation is. Lines that are close together show the steepest points. Lines that are far apart show flatter points.

How do people use physical maps? Hikers use them to find trails. A fisher can use one to find the deepest fishing spot on a lake. **Engineers** use them to plan roads and buildings.

Physical maps tell us a lot about Earth's surface. We can use them to find the tallest mountains. They show how deep the oceans are. We can use them to find a new camping spot.

How would you use a physical map?

DID YOU KNOW?

Photos taken from airplanes and drones are used to create physical maps.

QUICK FACTS & TOOLS

MAP QUIZ

Physical maps show us Earth's features and landforms. They also show elevations. Use the map key, elevation key, and compass rose to answer the questions below!

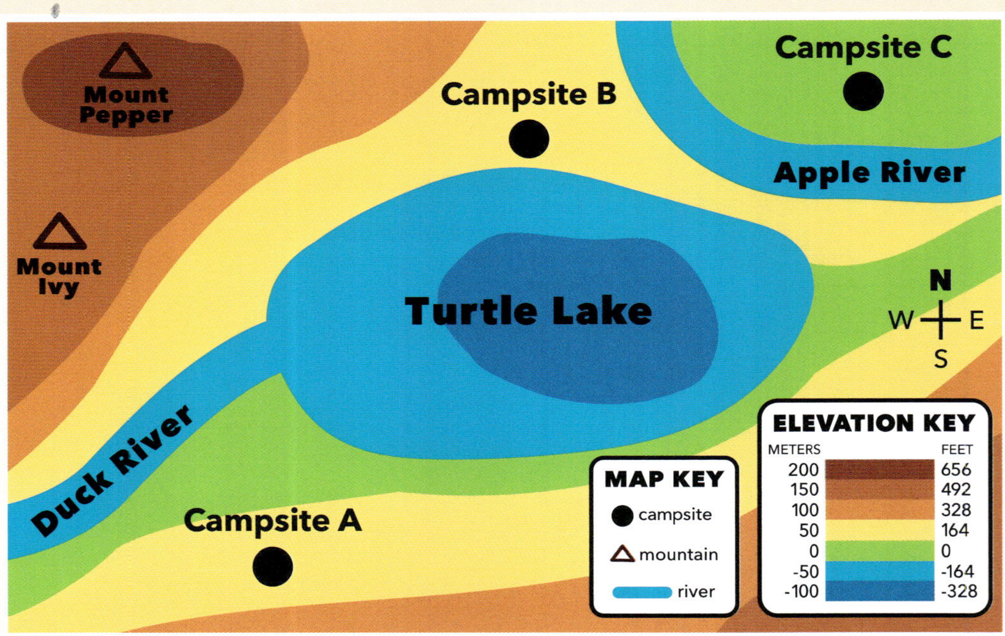

1. **Which campsite is north of Turtle Lake?**
2. **Which mountain has the highest elevation?**
3. **Which campsite has the lowest elevation?**

Answer Key: 1) Campsite B. 2) Mount Pepper. 3) Campsite C.

GLOSSARY

engineers: People who are trained to design and build machines or large structures such as bridges or roads.

features: Particular parts of something.

grid: A network of evenly spaced vertical and horizontal lines that forms a regular pattern of squares.

landforms: Natural features of Earth's surface.

latitude lines: Imaginary lines that circle Earth and run east to west. They measure distance north and south.

longitude lines: Imaginary lines that circle Earth and run north to south. They measure distance east and west.

sea level: The average level of the ocean's surface, used as a starting point from which to measure how high or deep a place is.

surface: The outermost or top layer of something.

symbols: Designs or objects that stand for something else.

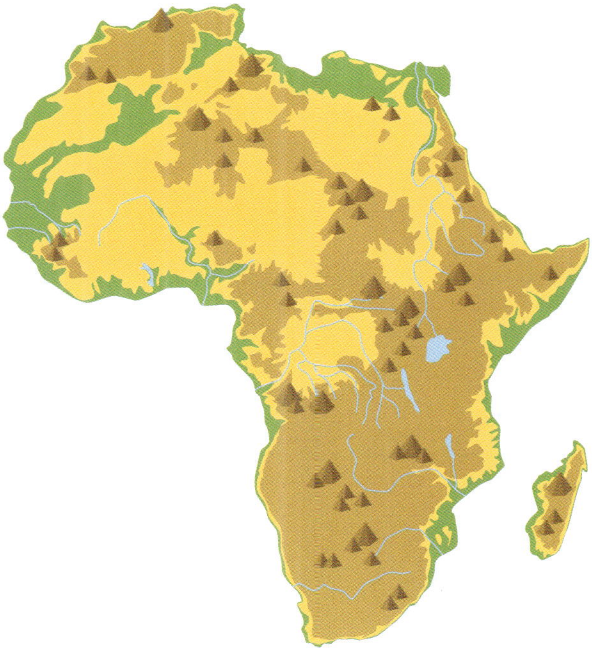

INDEX

TO LEARN MORE

Finding more information is as easy as 1, 2, 3.

1. Go to www.factsurfer.com
2. Enter "physicalmaps" into the search box.
3. Choose your book to see a list of websites.

FACT SURFER